FORD PICKUP TRUCKS

Steve Statham

MOTORBOOKS

First published in 1995 by MBI Publishing Company, PO Box 1, 729 Prospect Avenue, Osceola, WI 54020-0001 USA

MBI Publishing Company books are also available at discounts in bulk quantity for industrial or sales-promotional use. For details write to Special Sales Manager at Motorbooks International Wholesalers & Distributors, 729 Prospect Avenue, PO Box 1, Osceola, WI 54020-0001 USA.

Library of Congress Cataloging-in-Publication Data

Ford pickup trucks/Steve Statham
        p. cm.—(Enthusiast color series)
    Includes index.
    ISBN 0-7603-2024-1
    1. Ford trucks—History.   I. Title. II. Series
TL230.5.F57S73   1995
629.233'0973—dc20   94-44210

On the front cover: A 1953 F-100 is owned by Robert Campbell of Naples, Florida.

On the frontispiece: A 1958 Ranchero Custom, owned by Gary Gregory, Lubbock, Texas.

On the title pages: James Menke, of San Antonio, Texas, owns this beautiful 1941 V-8 pickup.

On the back cover: Don Scarborough of Blanco, Texas, owns this 1965 F-100 Flareside.

Printed in China

Contents

Acknowledgments

If ever there was an archetypal American vehicle, it would be the Ford pickup truck. Virtually everyone in America has had some exposure to the Blue Oval's big workhorse. My own earliest driving experiences involved wheeling grandpa's white Ford truck around the pasture while I fumbled with the worn out three-on-the-tree shifter. That was a long time ago, and last time I checked the truck was still in use by my aunt and two youngest cousins.

Like myself, everybody has a story to share about Ford trucks, or at least knows someone who owns a good one. I'm especially grateful to those who know where the good trucks can be found and helped me locate the pickups photographed for this book. Specifically, I'd like to tip my hat to Julius Neunhoffer for bird-dogging nice trucks in the Central Texas area, and Frank Reynolds, who did the same in Dallas. Thanks also go to the Ranchero club. My good friend Mike Mueller was also a big help in finding trucks and offering general good advice, not to mention picking up the beer tab a lot more often than he should have.

Thanks also go to Ford Public Affairs and Madeline Bullman at DeAngelo, Minton & Associates for help with the racing photos and other factory photography. Certainly, the most grateful thanks go to those truck owners who took time from their busy schedules to allow me to photograph their trucks. These new friends include: Doug Newton, Burnet, Texas, 1917 Model T military truck; Scott Lougheed, Buda, Texas, 1928 Model A Roadster Pickup; Richard E. Wunsch, Naples, Florida, 1931 Model A pickup; David Walters Jr. (with help from Gary Licko), Miami, Florida, 1935 V-8 pickup; James Menke, San Antonio, Texas, 1941 pickup; Steven Ottmers, Fredericksburg, Texas, 1947 pickup; Jerry and Donna Giebler, Gatesville, Texas, 1948 F-1; Hardy Johnson, Liberty Hill, Texas, 1951 F-1; Robert Campbell, Naples, Florida, 1953 F-100; Buddy and Millie Swindle, San Antonio, Texas, 1956 F-100; Wayne Turner, Lubbock, Texas, 1957 Ranchero; Gary Gregory, Lubbock, Texas, 1958 Ranchero; Don Scarborough, Blanco, Texas, 1965 F-100; Doug Bodensteiner, Garland, Texas, 1966 F-100; Buddy and Millie Swindle, San Antonio, Texas, 1971 F-100; and Robert Campbell, Naples, Florida, 1976 F-100.

Finally, thanks also go to Tom Wilson, because if there's anything of written or photographic value in this book, I probably learned how to do it from him.

Chapter 1

⋮

Early Hauling

By almost any standard, 1917 was a grim year. War had settled over the world like a dark cloud, and not even the oceans were safe when Germany announced unrestricted submarine warfare on January 31. The U.S. officially declared war on Germany on April 6, a conscription law was passed in May and by the end of June American troops were in Europe. For America, The Great War was no longer just another European skirmish. And anyone who was thinking of drowning their sorrows was about to get a rude jolt — in December, Congress submitted the 18th Amendment, dreaded prohibition, to the states for ratification.

It was against this backdrop that industrial history was made as well. Officially, the history of Ford trucks also began in 1917, on July 27, with the start of production of the 1 Ton TT chassis. In truth, Ford trucks existed well before that. Among the earliest Fords produced were truck-like Model C delivery cars, and individuals and small companies had been converting Model Ts into trucks almost as fast as they had rolled out the factory door. In a time when America was still discovering the possibilities allowed by automotive transportation, the Model T was a prime laboratory for experimentation. Self-propelled ambulance, fire trucks, taxis, hearses—all

The Model A Roadster pickup was the first of the light A-series trucks to be introduced, with the Closed Cab version offered later in the year. The heavier AA trucks received the first Closed Cabs. The pickup bed on the Model A was a hold-over from the Model T, until a new bed was introduced in 1931.

were in their infancy, and most of the earliest ones were converted from passenger cars.

The egalitarian nature of the Model T lent itself well to these types of conversions. The Model T's low cost and ease of modification made it a favorite among tinkers and entrepreneurs. Those characteristics also made the T a favorite of the military, and Ford would eventually deliver thousands of vehicles to the U.S. and its allies during the First World War. With motorized vehicle development moving forward at such a fast clip, it was only a matter of time before a factory-offered truck chassis would make economic sense to Henry Ford.

Even so, the 1917 TT chassis was not a complete "truck" per se, as it was delivered largely without bodywork.

FORD MODEL T ONE TON TRUCK

This is the Model T One Ton Truck just as we deliver to the purchaser, without body. The equipment includes hood for motor, front fenders, stepping boards, two side lights, two head lights, one tail light, horn and set of tools. All Ford cars sold f.o.b. Detroit

The official history of Ford trucks begins in 1917 with the introduction of the One-Ton TT chassis. Cab and bed type were usually supplied by the aftermarket and chosen and installed by the purchaser. The TT debuted at $600, but by the time it went out of production in 1927 cost-cutting measures had dropped the price to $325. *Ford Motor Company*

With no windshield, side windows, or doors, canvas was the only protection against the elements on this Army truck. The bed side covering rolled up into the roof section, while door and side canvas pieces were normally stored under the seat. The front windshield canvas partially covered the driver, but was little protection in rain and snow.

The U.S. Army and Allies purchased some 39,000 vehicles of all types from Ford before and during World War I. Model T pickup conversions built off the base chassis, like this one, were included in that mix. More than 7,000 of the first Fordson tractors were shipped to England as well to help with the war effort. The two-millionth Model T was produced during 1917.

According to James Wagner's *Ford Trucks since 1905*, Ford built 5,745 military ambulances during World War I, with the other vehicles supplied being cars and trucks like the one pictured. The "cab" and bed of this truck are wood.

The owner of this Model T was unaware of its significance until this serial number was identified as an Army I.D. number. The truck had been used for so long that all other clues to its origin had long since been destroyed.

But even delivered without a traditional pickup bed, the TT is significant in that it marked Ford's permanent entry into the light truck market. Except for a brief interruption during World War II, Ford trucks have been continuously sold ever since.

Those first trucks were simple beasts. The TT chassis was essentially a modified Model T chassis, lengthened from a 100in wheelbase to a 124in wheelbase, with a stiffer rear suspension for heavy duty use. The TT chassis included front fenders, stepping boards and a hood for the motor, two side lights, headlights, a tail light, solid rubber tires, a set of tools, and a horn. Price for the chassis, F.O.B. Detroit, was set at $600.

The engine was equally simple. The T's largish, L-Head, 176.7ci four-cylinder engine developed its peak 20hp at 1400 rpm. Compression ratio was a modest 4.5:1. These basic engine specifications remained the same through the end of Model T production in 1927, contributing to the T's well-deserved reputation for simplicity and reliability — although that product consistency would eventually lead to serious problems for Ford as competitors' trucks grew larger, more powerful, and better equipped.

Only 209 TTs were built in 1917, but sales grew quickly. By 1919 more than 100,000 had been produced. Sales of the regular T chassis, also still popular for light-duty pickup conversion, continued at a steady pace. Just as Ford practically owned the early passenger car market, the company soon came to dominate the burgeoning truck market.

In keeping with Henry Ford's philosophy of providing a vehicle the working man could afford, changes were few over the course of Model T and TT production. Although there were the occasional upgrades and improvements during the early years, most of Ford's effort was expended in keeping the price of the T and TT low.

It was not until 1925 that Ford introduced their first fully complete, factory-offered pickup — the Model T Runabout with Pick-Up Body, priced at $281. In response to increased competition, 1925 models incorporated other improvements, such as improved oiling and a 5-to-1 steering ratio. The TT chassis, at $365, was still the favorite for truck buyers, however, and both a Closed Cab and a Stake Bed were introduced that year to keep the TT at the front of the pack. Ford truck sales in 1925 hit their highest level ever up to that point.

From that peak, sales came harder. Although Ford operations were expanding in many different directions, rival Chevrolet had succeeded in taking a chunk of market share away from Ford. This prodding from a cross-town rival motivated Ford to offer a number of changes during the 1926 model year, including styling changes, brake upgrades and a retreat from the long-standing "black only" color policy on cars and trucks.

Truck sales were still strong in 1926, but it became increasingly clear that the Model T was falling behind its rivals in the truck business. A fresh model was needed if Ford was to com-

The Model T chassis utilized 12-spoke wheels with 30x3 1/2in Firestone tires on the rear, 30x3in on the front. The Army trucks usually carried spare tires on both sides.

Ford's first fully complete pickup, the Model T Runabout with pickup body, was introduced in 1925 for $281. That first truck was little different from Model T passenger cars, although they did use heavy-duty rear springs and brakes. Production was 33,795, but the tougher Model TT chassis was far more popular, with nearly a quarter-million units sold. *Ford Motor Company*

pete and stay atop the sales race. Model T production officially ended May 26, 1927, with more than 15 million total units built.

Ford's follow-up to the Model T began production on November 1, 1927. Dubbed the Model A in honor of Ford's first production car, the 1903

Model A, the new vehicle was introduced to the public on December 2. With a host of real upgrades, if few innovations, the Model A passenger car and Roadster Pickup were both an immediate success, as was the heavy-duty truck chassis variant, the AA.

Although still using some carryover items from the Model T, the A incorporated all the right changes necessary to meet buyer demand. First, there was more power. The Model A four-cylinder engine featured a 200.4ci displacement, and with 40 hp at 2200 rpm and 128 lb-ft of torque, was quite a bit more powerful than the Model T.

Styling was improved, with a more integrated look. The Model A was also larger than the T, with a 103.5in wheelbase, and the AA chassis offered substantially more payload capacity. Rated at 1 1/2 tons, the AA used a stronger frame, stiffer springs, upgraded brakes, and a stout worm gear rear axle. The AA's wheelbase stretched to 131.5in.

Of note is how the automotive aftermarket grew right along with the Model A. Buyers could customize their trucks with a virtual catalog of work-ready equipment. Speed governors, top rails, ladder carriers, compressors, winches, cranes—the list of available accessories was long, and deep as well. Anyone shopping for dump bodies alone could choose from offerings put forth by Best Body Corporation, Ed-

The Model A utilized a single, center-mounted instrument cluster. The shifter was a conventional three-speed, H-pattern piece.

wards Iron Works, Wood Hydraulic Hoist & Body Co., St. Paul, Palm Body Company, Inc., Hughes-Keenan and a host of others.

But if competition among dump body manufacturers was fierce, it was brutal at the truck manufacturing level. Despite Ford's ability to sell virtually every Model A the company could build, Chevrolet had moved ahead of Ford in truck sales in 1927, and kept that lead in 1928. Dodge, International, and others were nibbling at the edges of the truck market. The Model A truck chassis remained the country's price leader, and its reputation for reliability was unmatched, but it was also the smallest and least powerful of the major truck makers' offerings, in a time when the trend was toward higher content.

Early Model A chassis used steel spoke 21in wheels with Ford script in the center cap. Balloon tires were 30in tall overall, 4 1/2in wide.

Ford regained the sales lead in 1929, at the height of the good economic times of the Roaring '20s, but Ford's nationwide dominance would never again be assured. Between competition and economic depression, it would be more than 20 years before Ford truck sales equaled those of 1929.

Besides competitive truck makers, Ford was also still battling ghosts of the past. Among the literature dispensed to Ford salesmen were charts comparing the cost per year of buying and maintaining a 1 1/2 Ton Ford truck ($675 purchase, $270.21 operating cost per year) against the cost per year of eight horses and four wagons ($1,200 purchase, $1,292.64 operating cost per year, as per Department of Agriculture bulletin 997.) Even after millions of cars

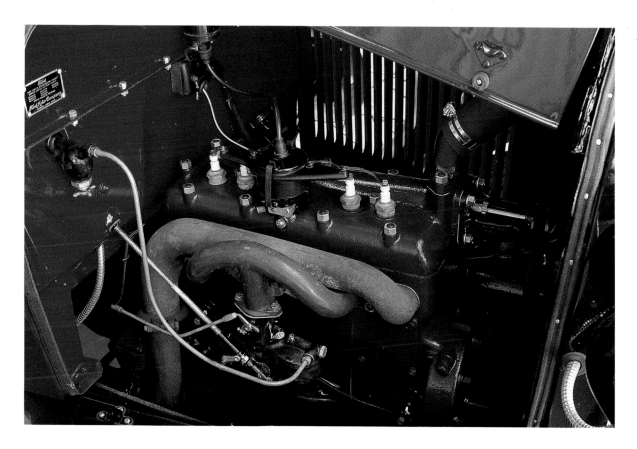

The Model A engine was a larger, more powerful version of the Model T's powerplant. Displacement was 200.4ci, thanks to a 3 7/8in bore and 4 1/4in stroke. Compression ratio was a breeze-like 4.22:1.

Right: Power output was unchanged at 40 on the 1931 Model A four-cylinder engine, which was becoming a handicap in the marketplace. Chevrolet offered a 50hp six-cylinder, Willys had a powerful 65hp six, and even the Dodge Brothers' four-cylinder weighed in at 48hp. Still, the economy and ease of maintenance of the engine endeared the Model A's four to many.

Left: After its introduction in 1928, the Model A switched to a separate parking brake system, with six separate brakes. Shown is a 1931 rear drum. Model AA trucks had larger 14in drums at the rear.

and trucks had been sold, the industrial revolution had not yet reached all corners of the country.

With 4,813,617 cars and trucks produced, the Model A was a smashing success for Ford, but in some respects the competition genie was already out of the bottle. Like the Model T, the Model A had perhaps hung around a bit too long. Newer, more sophisticated competition had overtaken the venerable A. Ford realized bold action was needed to stay ahead of competitors. And bold action would soon be taken.

Chapter 2

Of V-8s, War, and Peace

Until World War II, nothing had as much impact on the automotive industry as the Great Depression of the 1930s. Protectionist trade policies, plummeting stock markets, and drought-like weather conditions conspired to knock the wheels out from under the world economy, and more than one automaker went from selling cars to selling pencils.

And if the depression was burying the automotive industry, upstart Chevrolet was doing its best to dig a grave for Ford. Chevrolet had briefly wrestled away the trucks sales title in

Styling on the 1940 and 1941 (shown) pickup was remarkably similar to car styling, although the sheetmetal did not interchange. Differences between the 1940 and 1941 trucks are minimal, mainly wider hood nose moldings and other trim variations. This truck has the optional spotlight.

1927 and 1928, and Chevrolet cars, with their powerful six-cylinder engines, had eaten away at Ford's market share. It was in this climate that Henry Ford, creator of the automotive mass production assembly line, $5-a-day wage, and the venerable Model T and Model A, unleashed what many consider to be his last great triumph: the inexpensive, mass-produced "flathead" V-8 engine.

With Donald Sullivan, Carl Schultz and Ray Laird handling most of the engineering duties, Ford's new V-8 overcame the conventional wisdom of the time, which was that casting a V-shaped engine block was not feasible at the mass production level. The flathead eight-cylinder was also a public relations coup, as a V-8 had never been offered in any car that was aimed at the entry level car market. Not only that,

By 1935, horsepower on the Ford V-8 was up to 85 at 3800rpm. The previous year, Ford had made their first major revision to the flathead, raising the compression ratio to 6.3:1, adopting a two-barrel Stromberg carburetor and redesigning the intake manifold, resulting in the power increase. Engineers also addressed other shortcomings in cooling, fueling and durability.

Left: Nineteen-thirty-five was the best sales year for Ford during the depression era, no doubt due to the stylish redesign of its truck line. Ford regained both the car and truck sales lead, which it had lost to Chevrolet.

Left: Pickup prices started at $480 in 1935. The new body styling included sleek new fenders, a panel between the running boards and box, sloping radiator, and angled hood vents. The body was now all steel.

but the V-8 was brought to market in a remarkably short 18 months. Henry hedged his bet though, keeping the Model A's four-cylinder, in upgraded form, as the base engine.

The flathead "Model 18" V-8 debuted in 1932 at 221ci and 65hp at 3400 rpm, and was initially offered in the car line only. The engine had a 5.5:1 compression ratio and used a small single venturi carburetor. (Hot rodders wasted little time improving upon the flathead's breathing ability and compression, eventually making Ford's V-8 the hot set-up on the race-track and among performance minded individuals for some two decades.)

The new V-8 was destined for success, although not overnight. The depression choked off new car and truck sales during the engine's debut year, plus there was early customer resistance as the new powerplant proved itself. The early V-8s were not

Right: Steel spoke "wire" wheels made their last appearance on light-duty Ford pickups in 1935. In 1936 Ford introduced "short-spoke" 16in steel wheels.

Because Henry Ford was a true believer in mechanical brakes, his company lagged behind other manufacturers in introducing hydraulic brakes on its cars and trucks. Suspended pedals would not be used on light-duty Ford trucks until 1957.

without their teething problems, with oil consumption and overheating being primary concerns.

The V-8 became a commercial vehicle option in late 1932. Integration throughout the truck line didn't really begin until 1933, but the V-8 quickly supplanted the four-cylinder as the engine of choice. By 1934 total V-8 pro-

For 1940, Ford introduced what many consider to be one of the best looking trucks of the era . . . and truck sales hit a three year high.

duction hit the 1,000,000 mark. The four-cylinder was removed from the truck equipment list in North America for 1935, and in 1937 Ford even pitched an economical version of the flathead, the 60-horsepower V-8, as a good alternative to four- and six-cylinder powerplants.

But while the flathead engine changed the complexion of Ford's vehicle line-up, another factor was equally instrumental in jump-starting Ford's image — frequent styling changes. On the truck side, the 1932 models shared styling with the redesigned Model B cars of that year. The shape was similar to that of the Model A, but smoother, with a more integrated grille. The larger, 1 1/2 Ton trucks, designated Model BB, also received the new styling.

Ford cars embarked upon a string of almost yearly styling updates in 1933, which the trucks did not share, marking the first serious divergence of car and truck styling at Ford. But the days of long production cycles with minimal styling changes were gone at Ford. Trucks maintained the Model B appearance only through 1934. In 1935, Ford trucks adopted a look similar to that of the popular 1934 passenger car, with sloping grille, skirted fenders, and angled hood louvers. Trucks were restyled again in 1937, receiving a new grille and headlights integrated into the fenders. Yet another new look was introduced for 1938, the distinctive "barrel nose" design, which lasted through 1939.

For 1940, Ford introduced what many consider to be one of the best looking trucks of the era. Once again truck styling mimicked car design, although the actual body panels were different. The new look, new chassis, and suspension improvements introduced that year were received well by the public, and truck sales hit a three

Trucks were available with either standard steel bed, stake body, in Panel Truck form or dual-wheel chassis with closed cab. The standard box was 69.75in long and 44in wide.

The Power of Economy

Not so many years ago, an 80-horsepower engine was a big engine . . . heavy, cumbersome, costly to operate, expensive to maintain. But Ford has changed all that. The Ford V-8 Truck engine is so efficient that it develops over 80 horsepower . . . yet with all this power, it is light in weight, responsive, easy on gas and oil, economical to maintain. And today's 80-horsepower Ford V-8 Truck sells for a mere fraction of the price you would have paid for that same amount of power a few years ago.

That explains why so many truck operators . . . who have always needed powerful trucks . . . are changing to Fords and discovering the Power of Economy. It also explains why owners of lower powered trucks are buying Fords and getting the power they have always needed, but thought they could not afford.

Ford V-8 Trucks have been PROVED BY THE PAST . . . all over the world . . . in billions of miles of hauling and delivery work. Now they have been IMPROVED FOR THE FUTURE. Your Ford dealer invites you to make an "on-the-job" test of a 1936 Ford V-8 Truck . . . with your own loads . . . under your own operating conditions and get the first-hand facts about the Power of Economy.

THE FORD V:8 HYDRAULIC DUMP

80-horsepower V-8 engine with valve seat inserts, connecting-rod bearings of special composition, full-length water-jackets, dual carburetor. Full-floating rear axle with straddle-mounted pinion. Full torque-tube drive with free-shackled, semi-elliptic rear springs. Quick-action brakes. All-steel coupe-type cab with Safety Glass standard equipment in all windows. 1½ cubic yards capacity.

THE 1936 FORD V·8 TRUCKS

20 YEARS AGO THIS MONTH
THE FIRST FORD TRUCK WAS BUILT

FORD LEADS THE WORLD IN TRUCK-BUILDING EXPERIENCE

Today...

The first Ford truck was built July 27, 1917. Because it was built of materials stronger but lighter than those in common use, it combined ruggedness and reliability with low operating cost. Because it was sold in large numbers, its price was low. It was the first low-priced truck of quality, and it met with immediate success. Since 1917, Ford has built more trucks and commercial cars than any other manufacturer

... more than four million units. Measured in years or in units, Ford leads the world in truck-building experience.

Such experience has enabled Ford engineers to improve the Ford truck year after year. The 1917 model was 40 horsepower and sold for $600. Today's Ford V-8 Truck gives you 85 horsepower and sells for nearly $100 less. Road speeds of 70 miles an hour ... nearly double the speed of the 1917 model ... are possible with

today's Ford truck. Frames, springs, axles, clutches and wheels have been strengthened for greater load-carrying ability. Safety has been increased by the use of an all-steel cab and Safety Glass.

And as for ECONOMY ... today's Ford V-8 Trucks show the lowest ton-mile costs of any truck in Ford history.

Try a Ford V-8 Truck under your own operating conditions. Ask your Ford dealer for an "on-the-job" test of an 85-horsepower Ford V-8 Truck if your loads are heavy ... or for light delivery service with frequent stops, try the thrifty new 60-horsepower Ford V-8.

CONVENIENT, ECONOMICAL TERMS THROUGH THE AUTHORIZED FORD FINANCE PLANS OF THE UNIVERSAL CREDIT COMPANY

FORD V·8 TRUCKS

Previous page-Left: The Flathead V-8 engine was a major sales point in 1936, as Ford remained the sole producer of V-8 engines in light pickups. As the advertising of the time indicates, Ford touted the V-8's economy every bit as much as its power advantages. The company produced its three-millionth truck in 1936.

Previous page-Right: The Ford truck has seen plenty of anniversaries over its long life, starting with its 20th in 1937. On January 18 of that year the 25 millionth Ford car was built.

year high. Ford left well-enough alone in 1941, changing only minor trim pieces on the outside, although under-hood a new six-cylinder engine, Ford's first since 1908, was made available. Ford's four-cylinder tractor engine was also introduced into the truck line, although few were sold.

Despite the V-8's introduction and the bold styling changes, the thirties were an up-and-down period for Ford.

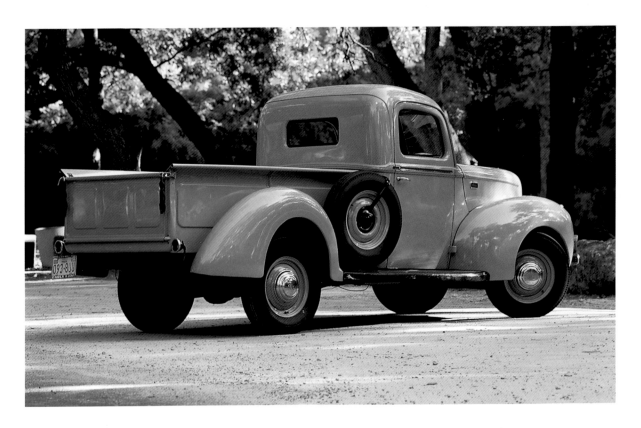

For the first time ever, Ford trucks were available with a choice of four-cylinder, six-cylinder, or V-8 engines. The four-cylinder was forgettable and quickly dropped, but the styling of the 1940-1941 models has proved more enduring. These models have enjoyed particular appeal among the street rod crowd.

The uncertain economy produced wild swings in car and truck sales from year to year. And after swapping the truck sales lead with Chevrolet on an almost yearly basis throughout the 1930s, Ford lost the sales lead in 1938, and would not gain it back until the sixties. There were several factors involved—not the least of which were strong offerings from Chevrolet and Dodge. Ford had also fallen behind in key technological

areas. Henry Ford had resisted the industry's switch from mechanical to hydraulic brakes, and it was 1939 before Ford trucks used the superior braking system—a full four years after Chevrolet adopted the system and nearly a decade after Dodge.

All of that was insignificant though, compared to the changes brought on by World War II. Even before the Japanese bombed Pearl Harbor in December

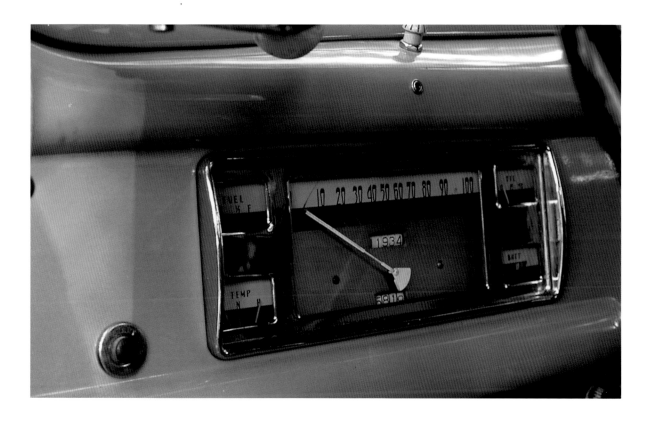

The instrument panel graphics were changed for 1941, reflecting an obvious art-deco influence. Soon enough, a military influence became paramount.

The distinctive "waterfall" grille is the mark of immediate pre-War and post-War Ford trucks. On most 1947s, the grille and trim were either all painted, but on this truck the owner has combined a chrome grille with painted trim.

Outside cowl vent was for providing interior ventilation. The driver's-side windshield wiper was still an optional piece of equipment.

1941, the effects of the war overseas were felt by domestic automakers. Strategically important materials became scarce, and more production capacity was given over to the manufacture of tractors and military vehicles for U.S. allies. When the U.S. entered the war, all production capacity was devoted to the war effort. Civilian car and truck production at Ford halted on Feb. 10, 1942.

The government all but nationalized the auto industry during wartime, rationing vehicles and materiél, and directing production to suit the country's war needs. Ford built a variety of military equipment during the war, including aircraft engines and Sherman tanks, but the company is best remembered for production of two particular war machines—the Consolidated B-24 Liberator bomber, and the "General Purpose" military vehicle, or "GP," or jeep.

The "GP" was originally conceived by the American Bantam corporation for military use. The Army chose the Willys GP design as the standard for production though, in part due to its more powerful engine. But to keep pro-

The 1947 1/2 Ton, virtually unchanged from 1946 models (which themselves were little different from 1942 models), was available in 6 1/2ft and 8ft Express bed lengths. The wheelbase on 1/2 Ton models was 114in, 122in on 1 Tons. Also of note with this bodystyle is the introduction of a Mercury-badged truck in Canada in 1946. The Mercurys used horizontal grille bars and other trim changes.

duction levels high the army requested Ford also build the Willys-standard GP. There was little argument from Ford, as Henry hoped to produce the all-terrain vehicle after the war—which did not come to pass, although by war's end Ford had produced nearly as many of the jeeps as Willys.

The B-24s were another story altogether. The Army Air Force realized that Consolidated and Douglas Aircraft Corporation, the two suppliers of the long range bomber, would not be able to supply the B-24 in sufficient numbers once fighting got heavy. Consequently, knowing the auto industry's great production capabilities, the Army approached Ford about producing the bomber. Ford complied, and constructed the huge Willow Run assembly plant, with production commencing in July, 1942. Late in the war Ford was rolling B-24s out the door at the unheard-of rate of one per hour, and the company eventually assembled some 8,600 bombers at the plant. The last B-24 was assembled at Willow Run on June 28, 1945.

With victory in Europe in May and victory over Japan all but assured, civilian passenger car production at Ford resumed on July 3, 1945. The cars and trucks produced that year were slightly upgraded 1942 designs, but were well-received. The United States was relatively unscathed by the ravages of World War II, and the American automotive industry was poised for a massive rebound as a large pent-up demand for automobiles needed to be satisfied.

It was a time of change and growth in America, with the wartime aggressors defeated and the depression long gone. It was a time of change at Ford Motor Company as well. Henry Ford died on April 7, 1947 at age 83. His death was headline news around the world, and even though Henry had retired two years earlier, it represented a new era for the company. Ford Motor Company was now Henry Ford II's concern, and he had his own plans and ideas....

Chapter 3

⋮

Postwar Boom

The postwar industrial boom swept along manufacturers of everything from printing presses to pacifiers, and many consider the trucks produced in that era as exemplars of a golden age of trucking. Ford trucks produced during this period are among the most sought after by collectors, and the styling is still appreciated and recognized to this day. Although Ford Motor Company was in disarray immediately after the war, losing millions of dollars a month, by the mid-fifties truck sales finally reached pre-depression levels and the company once again challenged Chev-

rolet for sales leads in several crucial market segments.

The spark plug for this revival was the first truly new post-war design by Ford, the F-Series pickups. Introduced in early 1948, the F-Series started with the 1/2 Ton F-1, progressed to the 3/4 Ton F-2, 1 Ton F-3, and continued through to the 3 Ton F-8. Ford trucks once again shared a common look throughout the line-up, which had not been the case since 1941. The styling was modern, distinctive and popular, and the public purchased more Ford trucks than in any year since 1929—although they bought even more Chevrolets.

Besides the looks, part of that popularity could be traced to the roomier and more comfortable cab. The new cab was taller, wider, and longer compared to the 1947 models,

The 1948 F-1 was Ford's first truly new post-war design, and was immediately successful. Ford also greatly expanded their truck offerings that year, moving into heavier-duty market segments. This truck has the optional exterior mirrors and spotlight, and the ever-popular addition of wide whitewalls.

Instruments were also new for 1948. Gauges included a speedometer with odometer, fuel level, oil pressure, engine temperature, and charging system.

with better isolation against noise and vibration. A one-piece windshield returned, vent windows were added and a larger rear window was made standard. A stunning new addition to the series was the 8ft F-1 Panel Truck, which was larger and had greater load capacity than previous Ford Panel Trucks.

On paper, the F-trucks retained many characteristics of the 1947 models, such as a 114in wheelbase and 4,700lb GVW on the 1/2 Ton pickups. Engines included the 226ci six-cylinder, introduced in passenger cars the previous year, and a revised, 100hp 239ci V-8. (A new 145hp, 336ci V-8 was introduced for F-7 and F-8 trucks.)

An automatic push-button tuning AM radio was optional on 1948 pickups. If not ordered, a block-off plate covered the hole.

The F-1 pickup did gain overall length compared to 1947, now up to 188.78 in, plus more overall width at 75.94in.

In 1949 the big news was the introduction of Ford's first post-war automobile design, a handsome car that wrestled the sales crown away from Chevrolet. Change was minimal for 1949 on the truck line, although an F-3 Parcel Delivery van was added to the line-up, and equipment options were juggled on the lighter truck lines. The story was much the same for 1950, with only minor changes introduced throughout the model year.

For 1951 there were changes aplenty, though. Among the more distinctive

Ford trucks ever built, the 1951 models were restyled with a more open, mouth-like grille. A single, argent horizontal bar supported by three vertical bars ran between the headlights, and the hood openings and trim sported a more aggressive look. An upscale "Five Star Cab" provided more amenities than before, with the Five Star Extra Cab offered as the top option.

Change was more than skin-deep in 1952, though. A new 101hp overhead valve 215ci six was introduced, marking the beginning of modern engine design in Ford trucks. The

Right: Patriotism and "Bonus Built" were the major advertising themes of the new F-1. Bonus Built was supposed to refer to extras Ford trucks offered compared to other makes and was used heavily through 1952.

Most 1948 models received a chrome grille, later years used a painted one. A chrome rear bumper was optional for F-1s. As most fifties designs will attest, the chrome shortages of WWII were a distant memory.

STAR SPANGLED NEW!

Hub caps at extra
cost when available.

Excitingly MODERN!
Strikingly DIFFERENT!

☆ **2 NEW BIG JOBS!**
Biggest Ford Trucks ever built! 145 H.P. engine!
Up to 21,500 lbs. G.V.W.! Up to 10.00-20 tires!

☆ **NEW <u>MILLION</u> DOLLAR TRUCK CAB!**
With living room comfort! Biggest contribution to
driver comfort in 20 years! New 3-way air control.
New coach-type seats. New picture-window
visibility! New Level Action cab suspension!

☆ **3 NEW TRUCK ENGINES!**
A new Six, two new V-8's! Most modern engine
line in the truck field! Up to 145 H.P.! High turbu-
lence combustion chambers! New Loadomatic
ignition! 4-ring pistons!

☆ **OVER 139 NEW MODELS!**
Widest job coverage in Ford Truck history!
Cab-Over-Engine and conventional chassis! Panel,
Pickup, Express, Stake and Platform bodies!
G.V.W. ratings 4,700 lbs. up to 21,500 lbs.

*Listen to the Ford Theater over NBC stations
Sunday afternoon, 5:00 to 6:00 p.m., E.S.T.*

Hottest truck line in history . . . from the
Leader in Trucks Built and Trucks in Use!

Our trucks are red-hot! That's because
they're brand new! Ford *Bonus Built*
Trucks for '48 are brand new in every
important way but one!

Big exception is truck-building know-
how! That isn't new with us! We've been
building trucks for over 30 years! We've
built more trucks and picked up more
truck know-how than anyone else!

From a combination of the NEW in
truck engineering and the KNOW-HOW
of truck experience, you get new thrift!
. . . new performance! . . . new reliability!
In Ford Trucks you get *Bonus Built*

construction, the extra strength that pays
off two ways. First, Ford *Bonus Built*
Trucks are not limited to just one job,
but are good all-around workers in
a wide range of jobs. Second, Ford
Trucks last longer. Life insurance experts *certify* proof that Ford Trucks
last up to 19.6% longer!

Drop in on your Ford Dealer to size-
up the new engines . . . new cabs . . .
new BIG JOBS . . . over 139 new models
in the biggest Ford Truck line in history!
*BONUS: *"Something given in addition to what is
usual or strictly due."* —Webster's Dictionary

FORD 1948 *Bonus* Built* TRUCKS 1958

BUILT STRONGER TO LAST LONGER

FE INSURANCE EXPERTS PROVE AND CERTIFY . . . FORD TRUCKS LAST UP TO 19.6% LONGER!

The Five Star Extra cab can be quickly identified externally by its bright window trim; on the interior the option brought two-tone upholstery, armrests and Deluxe door trim panels. The argent grille piece didn't survive 1951—on 1952 models the bar was painted off-white. This truck has a dealer-installed hood ornament adapted from a passenger car.

One of the benefits of the new-for-1951 cab was a 50 percent larger rear window. Taking a cue from the past, the pickup bed floor was once again wood instead of steel.

engine was billed as the "Cost Clipper Six" and was available in F-1 through F-5 pickups, plus some specialized models. It was nearly as powerful as the 239 V-8 in both horsepower and torque.

The modern engine's ability to nearly out-perform the larger V-8 showed that Ford engine design was moving forward rapidly, and the 21-

year-old flathead V-8 was nearing the end of its life. The final outing for the flathead in the U.S. was 1953, a year of otherwise sweeping change in the truck line.

If the F-1 set the stage for public acceptance of stylish, more comfortable trucks, the new 1953 F-100 brought the house down. The 1953-1956 F-Series trucks are probably the most beloved by collectors and truck enthusiasts and were enthusiastically accepted by buyers of the time. Extensively redesigned for 1953, the new F-100 was more rounded, had a wider cab than the F-1, and had more room inside. The new truck was more maneuverable due to a shorter 110in wheelbase and shorter overall length, and handled better due to the repositioned front axle.

Ford emphasized the "Driverized" cabs on the 1953 models, which was marketing-speak for a 55 percent larger windshield, longer doors with wider openings, a wider, three-man seat with no-sag springs, "arm-rest" friendly door side windows, a new curved instrument panel, and other features designed to make the trucks more comfortable.

Brochures promised "Every inch of these new Ford cabs is designed to free the driver of truck fatigue . . . to make driving easier, safer and more efficient."

Trim for the 1951 Five Star Extra cab included special wider hood side moldings. The following year the F-1 logo appeared in a circle at the leading edge of the molding.

Even more comforts were available through the Deluxe cab option, which included sound deadener, a dome light, door locks, twin horns, padded headliner, two-tone upholstery, and extra brightwork.

With the 1953 models, Ford began model classifications that would last for decades: the F-100 designation for 1/2 Ton trucks; F-250 for 3/4 Ton; and F-350 for 1 Ton trucks. The company also adopted a new crest for its truck line, a lightning bolt superimposed over a gear. Additionally, an automatic transmission, the "Fordomatic," was offered for the first time in a Ford light truck.

The modernization was completed in 1954 when Ford replaced the venerable flathead V-8 with a modern overhead-valve V-8. Known as the Y-Block engine family because of the deeply skirted block, the new V-8 made its debut with the same displacement as the flathead, 239ci, but offered more horsepower, 130. Also, the six-cylinder was enlarged to 223ci in 1954, and horsepower rose to 115.

Changes for 1955 were mostly limited to trim and appearance items, but a white-hot economy lit up Ford truck sales as never before. Although Chevro-

let was the biggest winner that year due to the introduction of all-new cars and trucks, 1955 Ford truck production finally beat the previous high, the pre-

Left: New gauge cluster for 1951 separated the speedometer from the other engine monitoring instruments. The Five Star Extra cab featured extra interior goodies such as a cigarette lighter and dome light.

Right: In 1953 Ford Motor Company celebrated its 50th anniversary and commemorated the event with special emblems set in the steering wheel. It was an anniversary worth commemorating—during 1953 Ford produced its forty millionth vehicle.

depression year of 1929. When 1955 was all over, Ford held 30 percent of the new truck market.

Despite that glowing sales performance, Chevrolet seemed to exert some influence on Ford truck design. When the 1956 Ford trucks were introduced, they arrived with wrap-around windshields, just as the phenomenally popular 1955 Chevrolet cars and trucks had. Ford also had to respond to the introduction of V-8 engines in several competitors' light trucks, something the company had not had to worry about for nearly 20 years. As V-8s proliferated in the pickup market, the Y-Block engine grew to keep pace with the competition. For 1956 the Pickups utilized the 272ci Y-Block V-8, introduced the year before in passenger cars. The 272 produced 167 horsepower and 260 lb-ft of torque.

Ford's percentage of market share dropped slightly in 1956, but sales

Probably no Ford truck is as admired after the fact as much as the 1953-1956 F-series trucks. The early F-Series were popular with customizers, and are as likely to be found modified today as stock. This truck has bed side boards, smaller 15in wheels and tires from a passenger car, and a chrome bumper with fog lamps.

The F-Series designations that would live for decades were introduced in 1953. The F-100 rode on a 110in wheelbase and had a GVW of 4,800lbs; The F-250 had a 118in wheelbase and 6,900lb GVW; the F-350's wheelbase measured 130in and the truck had a 7,700lb GVW.

Left: The 215ci "Cost Clipper" six introduced in 1952 carried over into 1953 with no changes. The six boasted a high (for the time) compression ratio of 7.0:1, and produced 185lb-ft of torque. The 215 was Ford's first overhead valve light-duty truck engine. This example is painted in factory rebuilt engine colors; the six normally came from the factory painted gray.

Above: A three-speed manual overdrive transmission was available in 1956, designated 3OD on the date plate. The bolt-and-gear emblem was standard on all trucks; V-8 identification was moved to the center of the grille.

Previous page: The 1956 Custom Cab offered a chrome grille, bright windshield trim, door identification, and interior upgrades. The chrome bumper on this truck is a custom piece. A Big Window rear glass option was also available on 1956 models and is actively sought by collectors today. GVW on the 1956 F-100 models was now up to 5,000lbs.

were still good, and the '56 models are considered by many today to be the most desirable of the mid-fifties Ford trucks. It should be noted that 1956 was also memorable in Ford history for the company's safety push, a marketing campaign that flopped among buyers.

If the 1956 models represent the end of an era for the traditional fifties pickups, the 1957 models can be seen as the first examples of the modern era in truck design. The 1957 Ford pickups were the first to employ the style of a flat hood with flush fenders; this style would be used on virtually all pickups for the next three decades. Likewise, the slab-sided Styleside bed

An option in 1956 was the five-tube AM radio with the "notched" dial control.

that would eventually supplant the Flareside bed in popularity was introduced.

The new look stayed largely intact through 1960, with the most notable changes occurring under the sheetmetal. A larger Y-Block V-8, the 292, was worked into the line-up in 1958, and factory four-wheel drive was offered in 1959. Ford Motor Company made aggressive moves in the big truck market, though. On January 10, 1958, Ford announced it was wading into the heavy- and extra-heavy-duty truck market.

Throughout most of the fifties, Ford and Chevrolet fought tooth-and-nail for market supremacy. By decade's end each had won several rounds, sometimes Ford taking the car sales title, usually Chevrolet taking the truck title. It was a spirited rivalry and would become no less spirited in the sixties.

The 1956 instrument cluster mimicked car features, with its "hooded" design. New wrap-around windshield from that year improved visibility and interior lighting.

EW FORD TRUCKS FOR '57

oldly modern styling...
odern through and through!

For '57 and the years ahead **FORD TRUCKS COST LESS...**
less to own ... less to run ... last longer, too!

If ever there was a year of sweeping change in the Ford truck line, it was 1957. Besides the new Ranchero, the F-Series trucks received completely new styling with the slab-sided look that would carry over for decades. Prices on the base F-100 started at $1,789.

Ford introduced a factory four-wheel drive option for F-100 and F-250 pickups in 1959. Prior to that, outside contractors handled four-wheel drive conversions. Among the best-known of these conversion companies was Marmon-Herrington, which had been closely associated with Ford for some two decades. Ford's system utilized Spicer axles, and a two-speed transfer case with a four-position shifter. *Ford Motor Company*

Chapter 4

⋮

Variations

Although the incredible popularity of specialty trucks and "sport utility" vehicles didn't blossom until later decades, the seeds of popularity for such machines were planted in the 1950s and early 1960s. Manufacturers started making trucks flashier and more car-like during the 1950s, as evidenced by Chevy's Cameo pickup and the GMC Suburban. More manufacturers also tried merging different types of vehicles, creating new market niches in the process. Ford's entry in this arena, the Ranchero, asked a different question—rather than make a car out of a truck, why not make a truck out of a car?

The Ranchero was exactly that. Basically a 1957 Ford station wagon with the wagon part removed and a bed added, the Ranchero offered all the comforts and style of Ford's new-for-1957 passenger cars. Sales literature exclaimed "More than a car, more than a truck—it's a completely new idea in utility vehicles!" Actually, the concept had already been tried, successfully, by Ford in Australia, where the car-derived "Ute," or Utility Ford, had been popular for some 20 years. Other, smaller manufacturers had tried similar ideas in America in previous years, but Ford was the first to make the concept stick—the Ranchero line would last until 1979.

The 1957 Ranchero was introduced with a 116in wheelbase, an

The "D" may be missing from the hood, but it's still all Ranchero. The foundation for the Ranchero was Ford's station wagon chassis. Ford's introduction of the 1957 car/truck hybrid caught everyone else off-guard. It was two years before Chevrolet would respond with the El Camino.

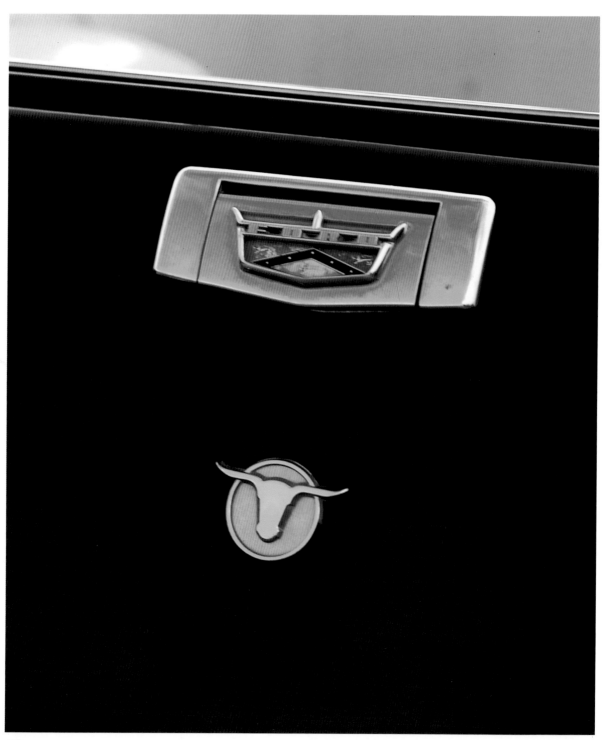

Left: The Ranchero received its own insignia on the tailgate. The hood ornament was the standard passenger car item.

overall length of 202in, a six-foot bed, and maximum GVW of 4,600lbs, as compared to a 5,000lb GVW on the F-100. There were three available engines: a 144hp, 223ci six-cylinder; an optional 190hp 272ci V-8; and an optional 212hp 292ci V-8. Some 312-powered models may have been built, although that engine was not listed in Ford's promotional literature. The Ranchero was introduced with two trim levels, base and Custom.

Public acceptance that first year was good, with 21,705 units sold, most being the upscale Custom model. But probably more-so than any other Ford truck, Ranchero styling bounced all over the map, first with

Ranchero styling in 1958 mimicked that of the new four-passenger Thunderbird, complete with quad headlights and non-functional hood scoop. Price for the 1958 Custom Ranchero was $2,236.

63

This Ranchero Custom was restored in the late eighties and is still in use as a business vehicle. Modifications include the chrome reverse wheels and dual exhaust pipes. The upscale Ranchero Custom can be identified by the large chrome and gold side molding and bright molding around the back of the cab and top of the bed.

yearly styling changes that mimicked Ford's car line, and then when the Ranchero name was shifted to smaller Falcon and Fairlane-based models. The first styling change came immediately, in 1958, when Ford attempted to inject some Thunderbird styling into the Ranchero. The experiment didn't work (1958 was also a recession year), and sales fell to less than half that of the '57s.

Ranchero styling and sales rebounded in 1959, just in time to compete with Chevrolet's answer to the Ranchero, the El Camino. The El Camino would be Ranchero's primary competitor throughout the Ford's lifetime and eventually would outlive Ford's car-based truck.

Always more car than truck, the Ranchero followed the car fashions of the day. After moving up in horsepower in 1958 and 1959 with a muscular 352 V-8 option, the Ranchero swung with the pendulum toward economy cars in 1960. Based on the new Falcon, the 1960 Ranchero shrunk to a 109in wheelbase and 189in in overall length. The sole engine offered was a 144ci

The Ranchero used the standard passenger car instrument panel. A speedometer reading to 120mph was a first for any Ford truck. The Ranchero interior was available in a variety of two-tone color combinations; the spare tire stored behind the seat.

Right: The 352 FE big-block V-8 was new for 1958, and Ford let everyone know with Interceptor Special V-8 badges on the glove box door. The 352 4-barrel debuted in the Ranchero at 300 horsepower.

overhead valve six-cylinder, rated at a whopping 90hp. The price shrank accordingly, to $1,882, and sales nearly equaled that of the Ranchero's first year.

Shifting the Ranchero in the economy car direction proved to be the right move, as sales increased to their highest level yet in 1961, and remained steady in 1962. But the Ranchero would not stay

FORD ECONOLINE. Saves on gas and oil, on tires, on parts—even on license fees, yet gives you a longer box and more rated load capacity than most ½-ton trucks.

Only Ford gives you a choice of three kinds of pickups

Get full-time economy that only <u>starts</u> with Ford's low price!

Now you can pick the pickup that best fits your need for maximum economy, rugged durability, car-like style and comfort.

Ford's full-time economy saves you money on price. Saves on gas, on oil, on tires. Saves on upkeep, too, with scores of special reliability features that guard against breakdowns. Only Ford dealers

can show you certified test reports that prove the economy of their products. Stop in today! Drive home a pickup that saves money . . . full time!

FORD TRUCKS COST LESS

SAVE NOW...SAVE FROM NOW ON!

NEW FORD STYLESIDE PICKUPS feature exclusive one-piece cab-body for smarter looks, greater strength and solid, fine-car feel. Also separate Styleside and Flareside bodies. Six or V-8 power, 2- or 4-wheel drive.

FALCON RANCHERO—America's smartest pickup! Gives you all the flair and fashion of a Falcon car . . . all its riding comfort and handling ease! Famous Falcon economy, too! Choice of two gas-saving engines. 800 lbs. load capacity! Choice of 3-speed standard or Fordomatic transmission.

PRODUCTS OF *Ford* MOTOR COMPANY

68

Left: This advertisement illustrates how many directions the pickup concept was moving in by the early sixties. The Ranchero, lower right, was now a compact, economy truck. The Econoline pickup, with its unusual forward-control configuration, was billed as a money-saver capable of working as hard as most 1/2 Ton trucks. The short-lived (1961-1963) one-piece cab and body Styleside F-100s were designed to make the pickups look sleeker and more car-like.

small for long. A 260ci V-8 was added into the line-up in 1963, and the entire Falcon line grew when the restyled 1964 models were introduced. By 1965 that 260 V-8 had grown to 289ci, and even the six-cylinder had grown to 200 cubes. The Falcon grew again in 1966, to a 113in wheelbase and 197.5in overall length. The 1966 model was a one-year-only bodystyle, as the Ranchero shifted to the Fairlane platform for 1967.

The pickup version of the Bronco was called the Utility model. The Bronco's pickup box was 55.2in long and 61in wide, an unusual case of a truck bed being wider than long. The Utility's steel top was removable. A three-person bench seat was standard, but bucket seats were optional. *Ford Motor Company*

Ford's Bronco gained respect among off-roaders thanks to the racing efforts of Bill Stroppe. Stroppe's Broncos dominated Baja and other off-road venues. Pictured at the helm is Bill's son Willie and future champion Rod Hall in a propane-powered Bronco. *Ford Motor Company*

The Ranchero's sheetmetal changed yet again in 1968, with the redesign of the Fairlane line. By this time the Ranchero had nearly returned to its original size, and the truck's economy car leanings had been supplanted by a more luxurious and muscular personality. The previous year had seen the return of the big-block engine option, and for 1968 there was a full-fledged GT package to go with it. Late in '68 the Ranchero truly joined the musclecar fraternity

when the 335hp 428 Cobra Jet engine was offered as an option.

The Ranchero kept its performance image through yet another restyle for 1970, when Ford's new 429 V-8 became the top option. The 1971 models were the last of the true musclecar models, as that was the end of the line for the 370hp 429 CJ and CJ-R, with their available "shaker" hood scoop, Hurst shifter, and other high-performance items.

The Ranchero was still married to Ford's intermediate bodystyle, now called Torino, in 1972, and continued to grow. Although a GT package was still available throughout the 1970s, stricter government environmental regulations and rising insurance rates had effectively killed the Ranchero as a performance vehicle. A 460 V-8, the largest engine ever offered in the Ranchero, was available through 1976, but it was not as powerful as the earlier 428s and 429s, and the marketing emphasis had shifted to luxury anyway.

The Ranchero became part of the LTD II family in 1977. The Ranchero did not live to see the 1980s though, as Ford's car-truck hybrid was given the axe in 1979. Ironically, in that final year, Ford sold more Rancheros than in the truck's debut year of 1957, but times and priorities were changing at Ford. The company was entering a

Ford introduced the Mazda-sourced Courier mini pickup in 1972, and Bill Stroppe wasted no time prepping one for off-road racing duty. This one, piloted by Carl Jackson and Mike Record, was photographed right before the 1972 Baja 500. Manny Esquerra would eventually win off-road championships in the Courier, but Ford's first mini-truck was even more successful in the marketplace. By the end of its production run in 1981 Ford was selling more than 65,000 annually. *Ford Motor Company*

period of massive losses and frantic change, and low-volume vehicles like the Ranchero were not part of the plan for survival. As an interesting footnote, Ford almost kept the Ranchero idea alive with a Fairmont-based "Durango," but killed the con-cept in 1981. Reportedly, 211 Durangos were built.

But the Ranchero was not the only unusual pickup to come from Ford during the fifties and sixties. One of the new niches that had expanded by the early sixties was that of the com-

By 1991 the Ranger was consistently in the top 10 in overall vehicle sales in the U.S. The Ranger eventually surpassed all Ford passenger cars in popularity except the Taurus. *Ford Motor Company*

pact van. Volkswagen's van had made a blip on the sales charts, and both Chevrolet and Ford responded with their own versions. Chevrolet launched their Corvair Pickup in 1961, and Ford waded in that same year with the new Econoline van and pickup.

The Econoline truck was a forward control-type pickup based largely on Falcon componentry. All Econoline derivatives used the Falcon's 144ci six-cylinder and were presented as more economical alternatives to conventional trucks.

The Econoline name lives on today on Ford's full-size vans, but the Econoline Pickup only lasted until 1967. The van-based pickups from Ford, Dodge, and Chevy never quite caught on, and by 1971 the last of them, Dodge's A100 pickup, had ceased production.

If the van trucks never caught on though, another type of truck-like hybrid did start making waves in the sixties: the "sport utility." The popularity of four-wheel-drive, in general, and International's Scout and Kaiser's Jeep models, in particular, did not go unnoticed by Ford. On October 1, 1965, Ford responded with the public

introduction of the new four-wheel-drive Bronco

The Bronco slotted nicely in size between the larger Scout and smaller Jeep CJ-5, and was available in Roadster, Wagon, and Sports Utility (pickup) bodystyles. The Bronco outdid its four-cylinder competition in the powertrain department with a standard

170ci six-cylinder engine but, like the Scout and Jeep, was still a pretty simple beast. All Broncos came with a three-speed manual transmission, a two-speed transfer case, and not much else. One advanced Bronco feature was its front coil spring and radius arm suspension, a more sophisticated set-up than what was under the Jeep and International competition.

Public acceptance was good, with around 20,000 of the small Broncos going out the door most years, about the same as the Ranchero. But the four-wheel drive market was a growing one, and Ford did not let the Bronco languish after introduction. The standard equipment list grew

As more people purchased sport utility vehicles for everyday driving, the product emphasis shifted more toward comfort and convenience. By 1993, Broncos were available with leather upholstery, anti-lock brakes, cruise control, and other luxuries once seen only on Lincolns. The base price was nearly $20,000, and well-equipped models bumped up against the $30,000 barrier. *Ford Motor Company*

quickly, as did the options list. A 289 V-8 soon joined the line-up, as did a dual master cylinder, side marker lamps (for safety!), and snappier interior trim.

The early Broncos also received a boost from notoriety gained in the racing arena. Long-time Ford performance hand Bill Stroppe took the Bronco under his wing and prepared several examples for off-road racing. These first racing Broncos were mildly modified from stock and didn't fare well under the pounding of off-road racing, but Stroppe soon developed the all-out racer named "Big Oly," thanks to its Olympia Beer sponsorship. With 1963 Indy 500 winner Parnelli Jones as driver, Big Oly ruled off-road racing in the early 1970s.

Ford continued to upgrade the Bronco in the 1970s, eventually stiffening the Bronco's body, offering a 302 V-8, and adding front disc brakes and an automatic transmission to the parts list. But the sport utility market was moving upscale faster than the Bronco was upgrading. Chevrolet's Blazer was clobbering the Bronco in the sales race, and combined sales of Dodge's Ramcharger and Plymouth's Trailduster exceeded Bronco's total as well. Ford followed the market upstream for the 1978 model year

with a new full-size Bronco based off the F-Series trucks and promptly sold more than 70,000 copies—more than the last four years combined.

The bigger Bronco proved successful for Ford, but the original Bronco may have just been ahead of its time. Ironically, on March 10, 1983, Ford reintroduced the small Bronco concept with the Bronco II, a Ranger-based sport utility very close in size to the original. Powered by a 2.8 liter V-6 and sporting a Twin Traction Beam suspension like the one introduced on full-size Broncos in 1980, the Bronco II achieved greater sales success than the original, if not the same respect among hard-core off-roaders.

The Ranger was introduced in 107.9in and 113.9in wheelbases, as compared to 116.8in and 133in on the F-100. The standard engine was a 2.0 liter four-cylinder, with a 2.3 liter optional. The Ford of Europe 2.8 liter V-6 was added as an option later.

Charting the changes over the Ranger's product life almost merits a volume of its own. By 1993, Ford's compact truck was the number four-selling vehicle in the United States, behind only the full-size Ford and Chevy trucks and Ford's Taurus. No longer a variation, the mini-truck has become mainstream.

Chapter 5

⋮

Modern Times

The truck division of Ford Motor Company made a number of significant product moves in the 1960s, starting with the redesigned F-Series trucks of 1961. The '61 models continued the streamlined, cleaner styling trend begun with the 1957 models, and took the integrated styling theme to new heights with a one-piece cab-and-bed Styleside model. These trucks were wider and lower than their predecessors, and moved the Ford truck line closer still toward popular car styling.

The 1965 F-100 was available in two wheelbases, 115in and 129in, two bed lengths, 6 1/2ft and 8ft, with either Styleside or Flareside bed, as shown. The line was also available in platform/stake configuration or chassis with cab. The Styleside was by far and away the most popular of the F-100 line that year, outselling the Flareside five-to-one.

As the decade progressed the company moved into other areas of the truck and utility markets, but the F-Series remained the big gun in Ford's arsenal. That big gun got new ammunition for 1965, with the introduction of three significant additions that would stay with the truck line for years to come: the "Twin I-Beam" front suspension, the FE big-block engine family, and a new family of large six-cylinder engines.

Twin I-Beam, offered in F-100 and F-250 4x2 pickups, was designed to combine the smooth ride of an independent suspension with the more rugged characteristics of the traditional beam axle. Or, as ad copy of the time declared: "Two front axles—wheels suspended on long strong forged I-Beams. Twin I-Beam is the first independent front suspension

• Front wheels operate independently, each on its own axle • Front axles are forged steel I-beams—like the big trucks use • Forged radius rods secure axles to frame siderails • Axles pivot in husky, long-life, non-lube bushings

'65 FORD

TWIN I BEAM
INDEPENDENT SUSPENSION

PICKUPS
BUILT TO LAST LONGER

Two independent front axles
share the shocks, smooth the road!

That's right, Ford's revolutionary new Twin-I-Beam suspension gives you *two* front axles—two rugged I-beam axles to share the abuse of the roughest going! And because of forged steel I-beam construction—just like big-truck axles use—they'll stand up in severe service! Moreover, both axles are secured to the frame with forged I-beam radius rods to hold wheel alignment, cut tire wear and reduce front-end maintenance! But toughness is just a part of the story. Independent wheel action smooths away road shocks...gives you a wonderful new feel of control...a new kind of driving satisfaction! Try it soon at your Ford Dealer's!

3 all-new engines!

Every 1965 Ford pickup engine is completely new! New economical 240 cu. in. Six is standard. Or take your choice of two optional engines: 300 cu. in. Big Six or 352 cu. in. V-8, the most powerful engines ever offered in Ford pickups!

78

with big truck durability." Larger trucks and four-wheel drive models retained the straight front axle and leaf spring suspension.

The Twin I-Beam setup utilized two, side-to-side forged steel front axles secured to the frame by two forged steel radius rods. Coil springs replaced the old front leaf springs used since horse and buggy days. Each front wheel moved with its own axle, producing a ride superior to that of most trucks available at the time. Ford promoted the Twin I-Beam heavily, going so far as to show diagrams of the system in their advertising.

To go with the new suspension Ford offered a completely new line of engines. On the lower end, the 223ci and 262ci sixes were replaced by sixes of 240ci and 300ci displacement. (The 300 six, like the Twin I-Beam suspension, has survived into the 1990s, exceeding even the flathead V-8's longevity.) The 352 "FE" V-8 replaced the Y-Block 292, giving the pickups both a horsepower and torque boost.

All 352-equipped pickups came with the new V-8 hood emblem in 1965, offering at-a-glance engine identification. Six-cylinder models used the now-traditional lightning bolt and gear crest.

The 352 had been sold in passenger cars for years — and the FE engine family would eventually make a name for itself with such high-performance monsters as the 427 and 428 Cobra

Ford wasted no time fixing the Twin I-Beam concept in the public's mind. Besides an exhaustive ad campaign, all pickups were equipped with emblems bragging of the innovation. These emblems only ran in 1965 and 1966, after which the F-Series line was redesigned.

Jet—but the FE was probably better used as a truck engine. With its heavy weight and good torque characteristics, the FE was ideally suited for heavy-duty commercial applications. In fact, the final incarnations of the FE, the 360 and 390, lasted in the truck line until 1976, long after they had been retired from automotive service.

Once these underpinnings were in place, the stage was set for a modern new body, which the Ford pickup received in 1967. The truck introduced that year debuted a look that would set the styling tone for Ford trucks for more than 25 years, with its character line running the length of the truck just below the door handles, large open grille, and timeless, functional proportions. These were the trucks that turned around the sales race against Chevrolet, finally totaling larger model and calendar years sales throughout most of the 1970s.

The look was updated in 1973, but not radically so, as Ford was not about to mess too heavily with success. That year did see the introduction of the largest V-8 ever offered in a light-duty Ford pickup though, the

Left: The 352 engine, introduced in 1965 and seen here in 1966 guise, was part of the "FE" big-block engine family that would become a stalwart in the Ford truck line. The 352 grew to 360ci and 215hp in 1968, the same year the 390 FE was added to the option list. Both remained available until the 1976 model year, after which they were replaced by 351ci and 400ci V-8s from the modified "Cleveland" engine family.

460 variant of the "385" engine family. The 460 four-barrel engine was rated at 239hp.

The latter part of the decade saw a push toward sportier models as the sport truck/four-wheel-drive/tasteless van craze was in full swing. In 1978 Ford

Equipped with a two-barrel carburetor, the 1966 352 produced 208hp, less than the 250 produced in four-barrel equipped automotive applications. But in truck applications, where torque is king, the 352 was never meant to

provide the high-winding horsepower necessary to be competitive in the car market. Rival Chevrolet's top pickup engine option in 1966 was the 220hp 327.

offered "Free-Wheelin'" options, which ads of the time defined as: "Free Wheeling means factory-customized trucks with dazzling interiors, special paints, trick wheels and blacked-out grilles."

— • —

Race wins show a dedication to high achievement but are still largely symbolic. Winning in the marketplace though, is another matter entirely, and Ford moved into first place to stay in the eighties.

The fun would be short-lived, though.

Possibly Ford's most serious revamping of their truck line occurred with the 1980 models. Ford spent $700 million to prepare the full-size truck for life in the eighties. After years of producing larger, sportier, more powerful trucks, two energy crises in the seventies forced Ford to

Although getting more comfortable all the time, 1966 truck interiors were still a pretty Spartan affair. Both left-hand and right-hand Armrests were optional. The panel at the bottom of the door was removable to facilitate window lift repairs, but a door storage compartment in that position was also optional.

go the opposite direction in search of efficiency. The 1980 models were lighter and more aerodynamic, although capable of carrying loads equal to the earlier models.

The 1980 models started Ford on a road of continuous improvements in efficiency and emissions control, prodded by both the market and the federal government. Electronic fuel injection became standard on the 302 (now called 5.0 liter) in 1986 and later spread to all truck engines.

It wasn't all so serious, though. The 1980s saw the domination of the F-Series truck in the marketplace, and eventually that fuel-injection technology would lead to the powerful 5.8 liter 240 hp "Lightning" engine in 1993. The decade was also notable for Ford ascension in another arena—off road racing. The creation of Special Vehicle Operations (SVO) in 1980 to oversee Ford factory racing efforts gave the company a boost in all aspects of racing but probably nowhere else has the success been so consistent as in off-road racing.

Off-road racer Manny Esquerra, in a Ranger, won the SCORE Class 7 championship in 1982 and 1984, the HDRA Class 7 Championship in 1982 and 1984, and the combined HDRA/SCORE Class 7 Championship in 1985, 1986, 1987 and 1990. Dave Shoppe notched a pile of wins in the 1980s in his F-150

The Twin I-Beam's forged steel construction allowed Ford to brag of big-truck toughness. While a sturdy system, over the years the Twin I-Beam earned a reputation for being difficult to align and for wearing tires faster than normal. For Ford Motor Company the plusses obviously outweigh the minuses, as the system has been in use for 30 years and has spread to other truck models.

Above: Standard safety padding on the dash was new for 1966. An optional Safety Package option also included padded sun visors.

Right: The 1971 F-100 Custom pickup did not differ substantially from the 1970 models, other than a new grille and minor interior changes. A short-bed Flareside pickup such as this retailed for $2,810 in 1971. F-100 4x2 Flareside sales were 10,106 units that year, a fraction of the Styleside's 332,131 sales.

and secured SCORE Class 8 championships in 1984 and the HDRA/SCORE Class 8 title in 1987. Ford trucks became more dominant in the late 1980s with the emergence of Chuck Johnson, Robby Gordon, Dave Ashley and the Simon brothers, Paul and Dave. All

won class championships in the later part of the decade.

Race wins show a dedication to high achievement but are still largely symbolic. Winning in the marketplace though, is another matter entirely, and Ford moved into first

The owner has installed a bed-mounted toolbox in this 1971 Flareside, typical of the type of work-ready modifications these trucks received.

This truck is powered by the 302 V-8, probably the most popular engine over the last two decades.

place to stay in the eighties. As of February 1993, the F-Series pickup was the best-selling U.S. vehicle for 11 consecutive years, and the best-

selling pickup for 15 years in a row. That's a legacy not soon forgotten and in that seems destined to grow for some time to come.

By 1971 it was no longer unusual to find air conditioning in a Ford pickup, continued evidence of the auto manufacturers' attempts to make trucks more car-like. According to the *Standard Catalog of American Light Duty Trucks,*

9.7 percent of 1971 light trucks were ordered with factory air conditioning. It is likely a good number of aftermarket kits were installed at the dealership level.

The first flush headlight Ford pickups were introduced in 1987, giving the trucks a more aerodynamic, if blunt, face. Upgrades were not limited to just sheetmetal changes though—Ford added rear anti-lock brakes that year also. Shown is a 1989 model, little changed in two years. *Ford Motor Company*

Left: In 1975 the F-150 (or heavy-1/2 Ton) debuted, Ford's response to stricter emissions laws requiring catalysts on trucks of less than 6,000lbs GVW. In 1976 new grilles were introduced. 1977 models, like the F-150 Ranger pictured here, were available with Tu-Tone paint and 351 or 400 engines for the first time.

Above: As more people began to use pickups as daily transportation, including hauling families around, the popularity of the "SuperCab" trucks soared, and is still soaring. The improved aerodynamics of the 1992 models, as shown, included a more rounded front end which led to better mileage and quieter highway operation. *Ford Motor Company*

Left: After a four-year absence from the Ford truck line-up, the Flareside returned for 1992. Undoubtedly Chevrolet's success with its restyled C-Series Stepside played a big part in the decision. The revamped Ford Flareside bed was more rounded than before, and was constructed of steel and a composite material. *Ford Motor Company*

From the humble 1917 TT chassis, priced at $600, Ford trucks have come a long way. Inflation and the addition of equipment undreamed of earlier in the century have kicked up comfort levels, capabilities and, naturally, price. A well-equipped 1994 Ford F-150 SuperCab, with four-wheel drive, metallic paint, air conditioning, tilt wheel, cruise control, 200hp 5.8 liter fuel-injected V-8, AM/FM cassette stereo, and various other bells and whistles rang the cash register at $25,318. Base price for the model was $18,571.

Ford teamed with BFGoodrich in 1991 to form an off-road racing "super team" comprised of F-Series trucks, Rangers, Broncos, and Explorers. Paul and Dave Simon, original Roughrider team members, were HDRA/SCORE Class 7 4x4 Champions in 1990 and 1991 and moved to the newly-created SCORE Trophy Truck class, an unlimited manufacturer-oriented division, for 1994. The Simons' F-150 is shown here at the 1994 Nevada 400. *Ford Motor Company*

Rob MacCachren joined Venable Racing and the Roughriders for the 1991 season, replacing Robby Gordon. After winning the SCORE Class 8 championship in 1992 and 1993 he moved up to the new Trophy Truck Series for 1994. Here he competes at the SCORE Fireworks 250. *Ford Motor Company*

Index